Take
A
Giant
Step

Take
A
Giant
Step

by
Pat Kedzerski

Pat Kedzerski
17 May 1985
To Lake Erie College

VANTAGE PRESS
New York / Washington / Atlanta
Los Angeles / Chicago

110302

6/13/85 gift of Gena MacFarland

FIRST EDITION

Published by Vantage Press, Inc.
516 West 34th Street, New York, New York 10001

Manufactured in the United States of America
Standard Book Number 533-03942-8

Library of Congress Catalog Card No.: 78-62932

I would like to dedicate this work to two wonderful friends, Jim and Gregg. Without their help I would never have been able to take that first giant step.

Contents

Take
A
Giant
Step

I. Self

Take a giant step—
Mother, may I, please?
Hold it now,
just why do you have to ask?
You're a mature person,
responsible for yourself.
You don't have to ask.
You can take that
step on your own.
There's no abyss ahead
in the dark
for you to fall into.
There will be stairs—
some up, some down,
but never too many
that reach too far
for you to go.
Take a giant step—
and then another,
and another, and . . .

Early February 1975

i am as the rising sun,
constant, yet ever changing—
radiating warmth, color, and light
to the universe
of which i am a part.

i am as the moon
sometimes showing my being wholly—
then sometimes shadowing parts away,
small, unobtrusive to the universe
yet to some, a light
that penetrates the shadows of the world.

November 1975

Sometimes
> I hear the world spinning
> 'round and 'round in my mind.

Then
> a vision of that world
> a minute particle of light
> a mere pinprick, yet so intense

Slowly
> it grows, its intensity becoming greater
> as each second ticks by.

Finally
> it bursts into a screaming nova
> the sky alive with the white fire
> consuming all that once was ours.

You ask what am I—
The things that I be,
First upon first
I can only be me.

I am multifaceted,
And if you look closely
Each facet is made
From scores of the same.

I am the extremes,
Yet I am also the gray
That lies in between
The black and the white.

That is laid down
Before me, to decide
Just where I am
On the graph or the screen.

The specifics, you see,
Can't be determined
As at one time or so,
I am at one point

On the plane, and
The next instant exactly
The opposite—or perhaps
A shade of the gray in between.

DIRECTIONS

up
disway or thataway
north
or
south
east west
crisscross

nne, ssw, nnw, sse
    east by northeast
south by southwest
    west by northwest
even east by southeast!
    but which way do you go?
tell me, I'm interested.
    aren't i your friend?
the times we've shared,
    don't they count?
the love we knew,
    is it all gone forever?
i see friend, it's still all there
    we'll still be close
and share our love,
    but we must, on our own,
choose directions

My world is closing in.
The time I have
is spent
doing something
for other people—
hardly ever for myself.
My brain pulsates—
a feeling of every
fiber being torn apart
by a being unknown.
Every nerve is alive,
electrically charged
to the point
where my body shakes
uncontrollably.
Soon I will be crushed,
then ripped apart only
to pick up the pieces
and begin again.

Drifting,
  my mind
    is floating,
      sailing
        far away
          in the beginning
            of the end
Through
  the mist
    to the shore
      where the
        end
          is
            the beginning.
A place
  where men
    trust
      their brothers
        and
          sorrow is
            nonexistent.
This Utopia,
  a dream
    i can only pray
      to reach one day
        when
          i am gone
            from this world.

23 August 1977

Surrounding shadows
Lost midst intellectuals
Shrouded in knowledge.

II. Love

People
Thoughtful, loving people—
Touching me in a way
Physically impossible
Swelling my soul
Lifting my being
To newfound heights,
Filling me with a warmth
That I in turn
May add my share and pass to others
Hopefully enabling them to be fulfilled.

22 October 1975

A YOUNG GIRL'S EXPERIENCE AT BREAKING UP

A searing pain rips through my body
As you calmly state your love for another.
My mind is whirring in an unfamiliar pattern—
Not understanding this sudden change.
A claw is grasping at my stomach,
My breath becomes ever shortened.
My body is wretching in sorrow,
Mostly sorrow for myself.
Why is it that I thought there was a chance
For me to find a place in your heart?
Why did I feel that your love for me was deepening?

Oh, God! This horrible feeling is getting to me,
It's getting worse all the time!
Why can't I be loved the way others are loved?
Must I always be a sister to everyone?
A buddy, a pal, a good whipping post—
Will this awful pain ever leave me?
I wish I were dead so this hurt could not reach me,
Search me out, hunt me down, and finally attack—
Torturing me, letting me suffer like this, chewing
    me up,
Spitting me out, casting me aside forever.
Will my mind always be this confused?
Oh, dear God! Don't leave me now!
Please don't!
What have I done?
I should never have hoped—
Why can't I be loved?
Is it my looks,
My personality?
Tell me, do I have bad breath?
Please, let's talk this out.
Please stay—
At least be my friend
And maybe the hurt, the tears
And the sorrow will someday fade.

Here we are alone,
The serenity of the forest
Reaches out and draws
Us into her bosom.
We sit on a fallen tree
And listen to the sound
Of water rushing in the stream below.
The sunlight glares through
The dense leaves
As you hold me close.
Never will I want
To leave this place.
The calm slows my mind.
Everything yet nothing exists.
Hold me and let me be renewed
In spirit and strength.
Nurture the spark
That exists between us.
Take me to the heights and depths
That only two can share.
Show me the heavens and the sea,
Take me to the bowels of the earth
And return me here to the forest.
Let me sleep beside you,
Rest my weary body.
Hold me close
And let our love grow.

You linger here
As the night fades into dawn.
The memory of our closeness
Still floods my mind—
The fury comes back as tenderness.
You touched me—
Setting my soul on fire
Taking my being—making it yours.
Together we shared the wonders of the earth and skies.
Again and again we traveled the universe
Causing the stars to burst—then softly drift together
      again.
The sun is rising as I lay in your arms
And the sweetness, the burning—all return
To be shared once again.

He is gone.
I try to remember
but his image
is only a blur
in my mind.

Without reaching
he touched me—
while I reached
for him and failed.

Now he is borne
to where I may
never again try
to touch his heart, his soul.
All is lost,

for he is gone.

The sun rose
as we sang
the last song
of love.
Dear to me always
will be the tempest
of the twilight,
the surrender to
the delights
of the universe.
As we part,
I remember the music,
the laughter, and
the bittersweet moments
we shared.

20 September 1977

I have lost again.
I gave my heart, only
To have it torn to shreds—
As it was before.
Why, why do I keep on
Loving and giving,
Only to be spurned?
I am vulnerable—
I trust when I should not,
I give too much.
I am alone in this world
Alone—and barely alive.

As I sit amidst the
autumn splendor I remember
just two days ago when you
held me close as we
said our good-byes.
I can still feel the coarseness
of your sweater against my skin
and the faint smell of
aftershave that mingled with
the aroma from your pipe.
How I long to be with you
again, to sit by the fire and
feel you so close to me, for
this can be an empty, lonely
place when you are on my mind.

The light in your eyes
is the light of the universe.
When they gaze deep into mine
I can see that you know
my soul
my heart and
my mind.
When you hold me close
I know that ours is
a love
that will never die,
for I know that you
would not otherwise
commit yourself,
nor would I . . .
I know your voice and
your moods,
your strengths and
your weaknesses,
as you know mine.
I want to be near you always,
in your heart and spirit,
for without you
I can no longer exist. . . .

GOOD-BYE

Why did you have to leave?
Good-byes are so final.
You enriched my life
with your vibrant personality.
You kept me honest
with your high moral standards.
You gave of yourself
and brightened the shadows
with your smiles.
I loved you.
I still do,
even though you are gone.
Good-byes are so final.
I shall miss you, my friend,
for death is the ultimate farewell.

4 April 1978

The breeze
ruffled your hair
as we gazed
across the ocean.
The sun was
a mere shimmer
on the water
and as we turn
our backs upon
its growing radiance

I reach for
your hand—
I want to
touch you,
to remember
the sweetness
of evenings past
when we watched
the last rays
of the sun
disappear behind
the mountains.
Ah, my love,
to live
like this forever
with the sun,
the moon,
the stars,
and each other
to hold—
I shall cherish
this moment always,
for now we must
hoist up
our packs
and begin our
journey home
to another
sunset.

Nights like this,
when I'm troubled
and alone,
are the nights
when I wish
I could run to you
and feel you
wrap your loving arms
around me tightly—
to protect me from harm.
I need to hear
you whisper in my ear
how everything will
set itself right
once more with
the coming of the dawn,
and how you will keep
my nights from being lonely.
I'm frightened and insecure.
I need your strength
to help me regain mine,
but I can't reach
past the walls
that are between us.
I cannot say to you
"I want you with me
tonight and every night."
I fear you would
think me foolish,
for I am but a woman
who, according to
convention, cannot

be the first to speak of love.
That does not change the need,
it only goes unspoken
until such a time
when you need me.

11 April 1978

The weariness
brought on by
the toils of the day
is vanquished
as you gather
me tenderly
into your arms.
I rely upon you
to restore my energies
for each day to come.
Every time you touch my soul,
you awaken feelings
I have never known before.
Since we found each other,
my world is complete—
I am whole.

My shroud of
loneliness has lifted,
unveiling a fresh,
new world.

III. Nature

The peaks of mountains
  Pierce billowing thunderheads
    A storm is brewing

Straight and towering
  The fir trees reach to heaven
    Grabbing the sunlight

26

Swift shadow
gliding the plains,
the hawk seeks
its prey,
its keen sight
noting
all movement
below,
searching
for the morsel
that will again
fill
the emptiness
of
hunger. . . .

A sigh of sadness
sweeps over the lonely pains
as the clouds hang low
and ominous—threatening a storm
before the day has passed.
A lone sparrow hawk
searches for the small game
that will fill the emptiness of hunger
it has known since the sun's absence.
The ability of distinguishing
night from day becomes increasingly difficult
as each hour passes.
Will the world ever know blue skies again?
Will it ever again see the sun rise over the plains?
The solemn cry of the sparrow hawk
notes the futility of his search.
His stomach will remain empty
until the creature he seeks
ventures warily out into the twilight.
The plain longs for a
warm gentle breeze
to caress away the chill.
Perhaps tomorrow
the sun will rise again
and all will be well.

The cool, moist earth,
mother of all—
calmly lets the
ingratitude
from those who
would see her
stripped naked of all
slip by—
those who have
chosen
to sever the
umbilical cord
between us—
unrelenting extinction.

See the eagle,
  Drifting, floating, soaring
    Above the trees,
      Child of the wind—
        Daughter of the sun.
        Proud, glinting wings,
      The brightness is blinding,
    Yet her keen vision does see the prey
  Swooping down, clutching a small morsel.
Contentment—
  Gratification—
    A full stomach.

21 March 1976

Warm breezes sail over oceans of grasses,
Bringing a sweet smell.
Birds dart and swoop in the air
Rejoicing in the renewed beauty
That has again graced the
Cool hard brownness of the ground.
Flowers slowly poke their heads
Through the moist earth,
Wanting to feel the warm rain.
Another winter has passed,
And all creation is awakening
To feel the oneness.

I step outside—
   Blinded by the brilliance
And feel the radiating warmth of the morning sun
   Against my cheek,
Cleansing my soul of all that is left
   Of the cold, gray night,
Awakening my sleeping spirit and lifting it
   To join the birds in flight,
Sailing and gliding against wisps of clouds.
   I close my eyes,
Drinking in the pleasant fragrance of the
   Tender shoots of new grass.
My being has become one with the morning
   Rising as the sun,
Free as the birds.
   Gossamer glinting in the wake of the new dawn.

January 1976

Walking through the forest
I search for the answer
That will change my direction, my life.
The calm and the coolness
Aid me in my quest,
Clearing my mind,
Freeing my soul
With the gentle wind
That caresses my face.
The answer will be found
Here amidst all that is nature's own.

Spring 1976

The blanket of
  snow is lifted
    and plants
      poke
        their way
          cautiously
            through the
              sweet
                moist
                  earth.

Strong winds
   dry the ground
      in vain,
         for soon
            the clouds
               will come
                  and soak
                     the
                        dirt
                           again.

Slowly
   the world
      becomes
         alive again—
            the little
               animals
                  scamper about
                     in search
                        of
                           food.

Spring is here!
   The joy of
      freedom from
         confinement during the
         cold, gray winter
            descends upon us
               and our spirits
                  soar to meet
                     the cloudless
                     sky.

26 May 1977

A voice
in the orchard
humming,
just audible
above the
buzz of the bees
working diligently
in the sweet blossoms.
What a reminder
of yesterday . . .
yesteryear . . .
ages gone by. . . .
The sunlight
streams through
the branches,
spotlighting
innocence
in that
small, humming form,
humming a tune
without rhyme
or reason—
but who in
the orchard
to hear?
Who to hear
the song but
those who
pipe a
tuneless

melody
themselves,
from dawn
until the sunlight
fades
into
dusk. . . .

23 August 1977

Bamboo tapping soft
Through the tender kiss of night
Rushes in the shadows.

A crusted-over
winter day
lies bleak
beneath
the gray skies
awaiting spring.

It beckons the
daffodils to
poke their blossoms
through the cool moist earth
that lies under an April snow.

The sun-dogs glint off
the pallor of
the clouds
in a sky-blue-pink
sunset—

A background
for the silhouette
of the trees
on the twilight
horizon.

Stars peek out
in a
darkened sky—
an ancient map
for midnight rides,

Some even daring
to flash
boldly
across the face
of the atmosphere

As they look for
a new home
in another galaxy
of stardusted
sunsets

That look down
upon glimmering
snow-covered fields
shadowed by sleepy
daffodils.

4 April 1978

incredible
is the
beauty of
the earth.
her colors
blend and
contrast
into wondrous
unique forms
that we
as humans
often take
for granted.
we tunnel
into her
depths and
mold
her surface
into
iron and glass
dwellings
with cement lawns.
who is left now
to remember the
mountains,
the clear streams,
and the density
of tall straight
trees
in the
vanishing forests?

The sky—
its usual chameleon self,
vacillates between
brilliant and threatening.
One moment it is
clear and unobscured,
with sunlight flooding
the atmosphere,
the next it is
filled with
unyielding clouds—
flooding of a different kind.
Night skies,
once brightened
by stars,
become illuminated
by streaks of lightning
that fence dartingly
amidst the scallops
of thunderheads,
cheered on by the wind.
              Another April . . .

Tines of pitchforks
rain down on me
in buckets of
cats and dogs.
The old man snores
while it pours and pours—
Chicken Little!
The sky is falling!
The evens are all at odds. . . .

Today I saw a rainbow
among the threatening clouds,
plunging into a grove of
pine trees from its graceful
arc in the sky.
It was so exquisite
that I was tempted to run
to its terminus where
I would surely find a pot of gold.
I knew, however,
that in searching for
the rainbow's end,
I would inevitably
lose track of its beauty,
so I stood transfixed
until the stormy skies cleared—
The promise was enough.

IV. Reflections

reflections
of my face
staring up
at me from
the image in
the water
the ripples
from a stone
blurring
the images
in my mind
my thinking
clouded by
the rush of wind
upon my face
i feel
the rushing of
the sea
pulsing
alive in
the wind
clouding
reflections.

Here I sit.
I yearn to learn
All there is to know.
I say, "Teach me, please,
But don't stuff my head
With so many things
That can't be retained,
There's only so much to
Be held in my brain!
Please be my friend,
It'll be easier for me
And prob'ly for you
If we can see 'eye to eye'."
Then, when I leave,
I hope to return,
To share with you
All that I've learned.

8 February 1976

To play a note
    Is but to utter a sound,
To expel a series of notes
    Is but a simple tune;
But add to this
    Deep, heartfelt meanings,
This is joy, ecstasy.
    It is Music!

Looking over a field
of cantaloupe seed
on a sunny-pink afternoon,
I saw lemon-wheel daisies
playing with the breeze
and the clover playing a cherry tune.

As I heard the colors go whizzing by
and saw the music they sang so low,
I dreamed of cotton-candy clouds
that I saw so long ago
in a world of wondrous peppermint streams
and the island of glorious snow

That danced with the wind,
the two as kin
the fiercer and fiercer it blowed.
And the road in the air—
the place that is where
the yum and the lollipops growed.

The sun that reached down
to feather my curls on
a rainbow of fantasy,
it comes back to me now
with the wintergreen swirls
of a beautiful melody

That drifts over the
field of cantaloupe seed.
With the sun far behind
I see that I find
that my dream world
really is real.

The line
from my pencil
that forms
an image
on the paper
in front of me
is not bold,
for i choose
to see the
shadows more quickly
than the defining exterior
of that which i draw.
The shadows,
the animations, are
the rose-colored
impressions of my
surrounding world.
Breaking the outer lines,
the colors of the world
run together,
muddling in the gray blur
of what is.
To corral these
beautiful free colors
back into their shapes
would be a sin.

Forsooth!
    I am the wanderer
    To thee I display my wares
    Of thy purse I rob thee,
    So, tender ones, take care!

    My medicines and patents
    Each guaranteed to cure
    All ailments and problems
    And "osis of the neur."

    My pots and pans—all made of tin
    The best in all the land
    But something I will never tell
    I got them secondhand!

    Good-bye, dear friend (whose gold I have)
    I'm off to make more sales
    The wanderer must find more fools
    to believe his fairy tales!

Isn't it strange
how the days
become shorter
as we grow
older?
I wonder
how few people
take time
out of their
busy days
to look at
the world around
them
and see
that it's beautiful,
no matter
where they are—
even inanimate
things
become alive
and express
their feelings.
The beauty of this
world makes me
loathe to leave it,
e'en though I know
someday we must all
pass on gracefully.

A lost soul
wandering through
the dark depths
of time—
The minstrel
has lost his
song
and
the lines
have strayed
from
the plane.
Alone
in the
vacuum—
Fog swirling
slowly
around and around
forming a tunnel
which leads
to a world
of peace.

The colors are
contained by
unbroken borders
in this world
of order.
Aseptic.
Sterile.
Cold.
What beauty
is formed
when the lines
are broken
and the colors
run together
side by side
as in a rainbow!
All men are
brothers.
Why must they erect
walls?
Why can't
they see
beyond
the borders of
their color
and let friendship
flow freely
so that this may
become a world
where no man fears
to tread
in the sea of color?